William
CAXTON

Damian Harvey

Illustrated by Judy Brown

W
FRANKLIN WATTS
LONDON • SYDNEY

Contents

CHAPTER 1
An Apprentice

When William Caxton was born in England in 1422, the world was very different to the one that you and I know today.

There was no television, there were no video games and no computers. There weren't even many books.

As soon as William was old enough, his parents sent him to school.

This meant that he was able to learn to read and write, something that a lot of people couldn't do. He was very lucky.

William had to learn French and Latin because there weren't many books written in English.

When he was 15 years old, William left his family home in Kent and travelled to London.

Life was very different in London. It was busy and exciting.

He became an apprentice to a
wealthy merchant named Robert
Large. He lived in Robert Large's
house and ate his meals there too.

7

Robert Large was a mercer, a merchant that specialised in buying and selling fine silk, linen and velvet cloth. William learnt all about the cloth business and trading with other countries. William was lucky to have such a good job.

In 1430, Robert Large became Sheriff of London. Then, in 1439, he became Lord Mayor. He was a very important man in London.

When Robert Large died he left William some money in his will. It was just enough for William to set up his own business.

CHAPTER 2
Off to Belgium

William packed his things and boarded a ship for Belgium. There, he made his way to the city of Bruges, the centre of the wool trade in Europe, and set up his own cloth merchant business.

He was a successful businessman and soon became Governor of the 'English Nation of Merchant Adventurers' at Bruges. He helped protect the business of other English merchants abroad in Europe. He also worked as an ambassador for King Edward IV of England.

While working as an ambassador, William gained the trust of the Duke of Burgundy, known as Charles the Bold. Charles married Margaret, the Duchess of York, King Edward IV's sister, in 1468.

Margaret liked William Caxton and she gave him a job as her personal secretary.

Even though he had a good job, William was still buying and selling furs, spices and other valuable goods. He also noticed that people were interested in some other expensive goods in Bruges…books.

Most books were written by hand and it could take a scribe years to copy out the text for one single book.

This made books very expensive. Only the richest people could afford them.

At first, most books were created in monasteries. As time went on, many scribes started setting up their own businesses.

Books were becoming big news and quite a few people had started selling them in Europe.

Most books were written in French or Latin. William didn't think that he would be able to make a lot of money selling them in England.

Then he had an idea.

CHAPTER 3
The Printing Press

William set to work translating a popular French book called *Recuyell of the Histories of Troy*. The book was full of stories of love, war and adventure in the ancient Greek city of Troy.

He spent days, weeks and months translating the book from French into English.

His hands hurt from writing every
day. His back ached from leaning
over his desk and his eyes became
red and sore from staring at the
pages for so long.

He was ready to give up, but
Margaret, the Duchess of Burgundy,
persuaded him to keep going.

When it was finished, the book became very popular in the Duke's royal court and people couldn't wait to read it. They all wanted a copy of the book for themselves, and they wanted it now!

William knew that it would take him the rest of his life to write enough copies of the book, but he had heard there was a faster way of doing it.

Someone in Germany had made a machine that could make books very quickly.

Caxton was determined to find out all about it. He packed his bags and set off for the German city of Cologne.

A few years earlier, a goldsmith named Johannes Gutenberg had been working on something that would completely change the way that books were made in Europe.

Gutenberg's invention used a mixture of old and new technology from around the world. He used paper from China, metal letters cast in Europe, a large wooden screw from German wine presses and ink.

He used his invention to print copies of the Bible in Latin. It proved very popular and people couldn't wait to buy one. But Gutenberg never made much money from his invention.

Caxton stayed in Cologne and learned all about printing and how to use the printing press.

Instead of spending a year or more copying a single book, the printing press could print hundreds of books in just a few weeks… and each one looked the same.

They look perfect!

William Caxton was so impressed
with the printing press that he
bought one for himself and took it
back to Bruges.

Unlike Gutenberg, Caxton was sure
he would be able to make a lot of
money from printing books.

CHAPTER 4
A London Bookshop

When he arrived in Bruges, Caxton didn't waste any time. He set up his printing press and got to work publishing copies of the book that he had spent so long translating.

Recuyell of the Histories of Troy was the first book ever to be printed in the English language. It was a great success.

William had not forgotten all the work he had done as a merchant. He knew how important it was to make things look attractive. He had new styles of print created that his readers would like.

He soon got to work translating and printing his second book, *The Play of Chess*. This was the first of Caxton's books to be dated – 1474. It was also the first book have a dedication inside.

To the right honourable

Prince George
Duke of Clarence

Caxton was happy with the way his new publishing business was going, but he couldn't help thinking it would be even more successful somewhere else. Luckily, he knew just the place to go…

In 1476, William Caxton packed his bags and his printing press, and returned to London. There, in a small room in Westminster Abbey, he set up the first printing press in England.

By printing books in English, and making them cheaper to buy, it meant that more people could have them. It also meant that ideas and information could be spread from person to person, and place to place, very quickly.

It was an exciting time and the beginning of a new era – the revolution of the word. Books beame more and more popular.

Before, only very rich people could afford to buy books. Now, books were becoming available to poorer people too. But some rich people didn't think it was a good idea for the poor to learn too much.

They wanted books to be just for the rich. Caxton wanted to make books for everyone.

CHAPTER 5
Books, Books, Books!

A lot of books Caxton published were ones he had translated himself, but the book he is most famous for printing was written by an English poet called Geoffrey Chaucer.

Chaucer had died before Caxton was born, but his book, *The Canterbury Tales,* was already popular. Caxton was sure he could sell lots of copies of the book if he printed it, and he was right.

Caxton printed *The Canterbury Tales* in 1476 and lots of people bought it from his bookshop in Westminster Abbey. It was the first bookshop in England.

Unlike other printers at the time, Caxton was a businessman and wanted to print books that people would buy. He liked the thought of making lots of money.

In his life, he printed over one hundred books. Many of them were written by popular authors and told tales of romance and adventure.

He was the first person to print an illustrated book, *The Mirror of the World*. He also printed Sir Thomas Mallory's stories of King Arthur.

Caxton died in 1492 and was buried in St Margaret's Church near Westminster Abbey. This wasn't the end of his printing business though.

His assistant, Wynkyn de Worde, carried on printing even more books.

Books became so popular that more and more people wanted to learn to read. They also helped spread an English language that everyone in the country could understand.

In 1954, a plaque was put on the wall in Poet's Corner in Westminster Abbey, London. It tells everyone that Caxton had set up his printing press there and how important he was.

1476

NEAR THIS PLACE
WILLIAM CAXTON
SET UP
THE FIRST
PRINTING PRESS
IN
ENGLAND

Today, the British Library receives a copy of every book that is printed in the English language, including this one, and there are over 625 kilometres of bookshelves. It all exists thanks to William Caxton.

Timeline

1422   William Caxton is born in Kent, England.

1437   Caxton becomes an apprentice to Robert Large.

1441   Caxton goes to Bruges in Belgium and sets up his own merchant cloth business.

1450   Johannes Gutenberg invents the movable type printing press.

1461   Edward IV becomes King of England

1463   Caxton becomes Governor

of the 'English Nation of Merchant Adventurers'.

1470 Caxton visits Cologne in Germany to learn about printing books.

1473 *The Recuyell of the Histories of Troy* is the first book to printed in the English language.

1476 Caxton returns to England and sets up a printing press in Westminster Abbey, London.

1483 Caxton publishes an illustrated version of *The Canterbury Tales*.

1492 Caxton dies and is buried in St Margaret's Church, Westminster, London.

First published in 2014 by
Franklin Watts
338 Euston Road
London NW1 3BH

Franklin Watts Australia
Level 17/207 Kent Street
Sydney NSW 2000

HB ISBN 978 1 4451 3310 2
PB ISBN 978 1 4451 3312 6
Library ebook ISBN 978 1 4451 3319 5
ebook ISBN 978 1 4451 3321 8

Dewey Decimal Classification Number: 686.2'092

Series editor: Melanie Palmer
Series designer Cathryn Gilbert

Printed in Great Britain

Franklin Watts is a division of Hachette Children's Books,
an Hachette UK company.
www.hachette.co.uk